THE ABDUCTION PREVENTION LIBRARY™

STAYING SAFE AT HOME AND ON-LINE

Cynthia MacGregor

The Rosen Publishing Group's
PowerKids Press™
New York

Published in 1999 by The Rosen Publishing Group, Inc.
29 East 21st Street, New York, NY 10010

First Edition

Book Design: Danielle Primiceri

Photo Illustrations: Cover Seth Dinnerman; pp.4, 8, 11, 12, 15, 16, 19, 20 © Seth Dinnerman; p. 7 © Sarah Freedman

MacGregor, Cynthia.
    Staying safe at home and on-line/ by Cynthia MacGregor.
        p.   cm. — (The abduction prevention library)
    Summary: Offers advice about how to remain safe when home alone as well as how to protect oneself from potentially dangerous situations online.
    ISBN 0-8239-5251-7
    1. Safety education—Juvenile literature. 2. Children—Crimes against—Prevention—Juvenile literature. 3. Children and strangers—Juvenile literature. 4. Internet (Computer network) and children—Juvenile literature. [1.Safety.] I. Title. II. Series.
HV6250.4.C48M33 1997
613.6—dc21   97-47364
                                                                                                      CIP
                                                                                                      AC

Manufactured in the United States of America

Contents

Home Safe

Do you and your friends play hide-and-seek? Do you yell "Home safe!" when you touch home base? It's no wonder. Home—your real home—is where you feel safe and **secure** (sih-KYUR).

But what if you're home alone? Or what if you're on-line? Your home and on-line can be safe places. But sometimes bad people can try to meet you in these places. It is important to know how to be safe when you are home alone or on-line.

◀ *It's easier to have fun when you're feeling safe.*

A Very Important Job

When you're home alone, you're in charge. You're in charge of keeping yourself safe. A big part of being home alone is knowing whether to open the door. Did Mom tell you she was expecting a package? She can ask your neighbor to **accept** (ak-SEPT) it for her. Did she say that someone was coming to fix the sink? She can call ahead of time and figure out another time for someone to fix it. Part of being in charge when you're home alone is working out a plan with your mom or dad that will help you stay in charge and stay safe.

You and your parent can talk about what is safe ▶
for you to do when you're home alone.

When White Lies Are Smart Lies

Suppose someone you don't know calls on the phone or rings the doorbell while you're home alone. Be smart: Don't answer the door for anyone you don't know. Don't worry about missing an important person at the door. If it's important, the person can come back when your mom or dad is home. If the person won't go away, call a neighbor that your family trusts. If the neighbor isn't home, call 911.

If someone calls on the phone, don't tell the person that your parents aren't home. Say that Mom or Dad is in the shower or taking a nap.

◀ *Keep the door locked even if you think the person at the door has left.*

You're Not in Trouble

Suppose your next door neighbor rings the doorbell while you're home alone. She's a nice neighbor. Your mom likes her, and you like her too. Will your mom be angry with you for not letting the neighbor into the house?

No way! You won't get into trouble for not letting someone inside. In fact, you could put yourself in danger if you do let in the wrong person. Talk to your parents about it. Ask them if you should let friends and neighbors into the house when you're alone, which neighbors and friends are safe, and which ones are not safe.

Your parents might tell you to not answer the door at all when you're home alone. ▶

Doing the Right Thing

A neighbor wanted to leave something for Keith's mom. But Keith didn't want to let her in the house. The neighbor didn't understand. "You know me, Keith!" she said.

Did Keith do the right thing? You bet he did. It's more important to stay safe than to worry about what a neighbor wants. Don't feel **guilty** (GIL-tee) about upsetting someone. Your neighbor can always come back later. And good people will understand and **respect** (re-SPEKT) that you are trying to stay safe.

◀ *Even if you have to stand on a chair to do it, use the peephole in your door to see who is there.*

Don't Be Fooled

Sometimes bad people do things we don't understand. For example, a bad person may pretend to be a good person, such as a police officer. But you can take steps to stay safe from these people.

If someone comes to the door and says she's a police officer, don't open the door. Call a neighbor that your parent trusts. Ask the neighbor to come over and make sure that the person really is a police officer. If the neighbor isn't home, ask the officer to come back later. If she doesn't leave, call 911.

A real police officer will understand why you might ▶
call a neighbor for help before opening the door.

Liars On-line

It's too bad that some people like to tell lies. It can happen at school and at home. But people can also tell lies on-line.

When you're typing messages on your computer to another person, you don't know who is at the other end. A person who says he's a boy named Rob could really be a girl named Robin. A man could even pretend to be a woman.

Don't give your last name, address, or your phone number to anyone on-line. Make sure a grown-up knows when you're using the computer.

Being on-line can be fun, but you still need to be careful.

17

Sarah

Sometimes Sarah gets homework help from the Internet. Her mom taught her how to find out all kinds of things by using the computer. One day, Sarah got on the Internet for help with a class project. She went on-line and saw something that said "Make Friends! Have Fun!" Sarah always liked to make new friends and have fun, so she went into the program. Soon, someone named Ray was asking how old she was. He also wanted to know where she lived. Sarah didn't like these questions. She ran to tell her mom. "You did the right thing," Mom said.

Trying new things on the Internet with your mom or dad is the safe and smart way to go. ▶

Dangers On-line

There are people who go on-line just to hurt other people. And, often, the people they want to hurt are kids. Many nice, honest people will ask you what you look like while you're on-line. But so will many bad people. A bad person may ask you other questions that could make you feel uncomfortable. If anyone asks you questions or types something on-line that gives you an uncomfortable feeling, don't answer the person. Tell your parents right away.

◄ *You can tell your parents about anything that makes you uncomfortable, even if you may think it's not important.*

Being Smart

Did someone on the phone ask you a lot of questions? Did a neighbor try to make you open the door for her when you were home alone? Whether you were in one of these **situations** (sit-choo-AY-shunz) or not, now you know what you can do to keep yourself safe if you're ever home alone or on-line. You also know that you should tell your parents about any situation that makes you feel uncomfortable. Be smart and keep yourself safe!

Glossary

accept (ak-SEPT) To recognize something as the way it is.

guilty (GIL-tee) How a person feels when she thinks she
    has done something wrong.

respect (re-SPEKT) To think highly of someone.

secure (sih-KYUR) To feel safe and protected.

situation (sit-choo-AY-shun) A problem; an event that
    happens.

Index

QUAKERTOWN ELEMENTARY
SCHOOL LIBRARY
123 S 7th Street
Quakertown, Pa.   18951

1. Books may be kept for one week, and may be renewed once for the same period.
2. A fine is charged for each day a book is kept beyond the due date.
3. Books damaged beyond reasonable wear shall be paid for.